Introduction

During 2017 members of the Newton Road United Reformed Church, Great Barr voted to close their church at the end of the year. The United Reformed Church West Midlands Trust had undertaken a detailed survey and concluded that there was a need for extensive and costly repairs to ensure the building was safe. The Elders were asked to provide an "action plan" or "all must reconsider the viability of continuing to operate from this building."[1] The cost of these repairs was way beyond the means of the remaining congregation and they felt they had no alternative but to close.[2]

For the time being, this brings to an end the proud history of non-conformist worship in Newton. However, since the 1750s there have been successive non-conformist churches and congregations in the neighbourhood and may well be again in the future.

This short booklet tells the story of the modern-day congregation that has met since 1917, but also tells the story of earlier generations that had a vision to serve God in Newton.

---

[1] Letter from United Reformed Church (West Midlands) Trust Limited to Elders, 26 January 2017.
[2] Letter from Elders to visiting preachers, October 2017.

3

The early years

The Newton Road United Reformed Church was formally established in 1917 as a Congregational Church. It moved to its final location in 1932.

In 1917 Newton was a small hamlet on the west side of the sprawling parish of Barr, or Great Barr, which lay either side of the Birmingham to Walsall road. Nineteen farms were listed in the parish and two places of worship, an Anglican Church and a Methodist Chapel, both a 25 and 40-minute walk from Newton. The main occupation was farming with the chief crops being wheat and roots. The census of 1911 had identified a population of 1,657[3]. This was an increase on the 1901 population of 1,344.[4] By 1921 the population had grown to 2,232.[5] Newton faced gradual urban encroachment from the large towns around it such as Birmingham, Walsall and West Bromwich. The most immediate example would have been to the south following the opening of the Hamstead colliery in 1875 which led to the creation of a mining community.[6]

The roots of the congregation extend back to the tiny cottage by the Malt Shovel public house which had been occupied by Joseph and Elizabeth Asbury and their

---

[3] *Kelly's Directory for Staffordshire 1916*, entry for Barr, London, 1916.
[4] *Kelly's Directory for Staffordshire 1912*, entry for Barr, London, 1912.
[5] *Kelly's Directory for Staffordshire 1924*, entry for Barr, London, 1924.
[6] *Hamstead Miners Memorial Trust* website, http://miners.b43.co.uk/history.html, downloaded 29 November 2017.

two children from about 1747. Their daughter Sarah died soon after. This had a profound effect on Elizabeth which was only relieved when an evangelistic Methodist or Baptist "opened her eyes". Soon the atmosphere in the cottage changed dramatically. The surviving son, Francis, became an enthusiastic preacher and eventually built up the Methodist Church in the colonial and post-revolutionary United States. Joseph and Elizabeth stayed in the cottage and created a congregation which met for more than half a century.[7]

Joseph died in 1798 and Elizabeth in 1802. It appears that the congregation of 19 continued to meet, possibly in the cottage. By 1808 they were able to erect a small chapel opposite the original Malt Shovel public house on Newton Road, on the east corner with Hamstead Road. By 1811 the congregation had fallen to 14 and thereafter it disappeared from the Methodist circuit records. In 1823 the chapel was bought by the Congregationalists and several of their eminent preachers including Robert Dale, preached there.[8]

The Congregationalist cause continued for much of the nineteenth century. The chapel had seating for 125. In 1850 it was recorded that 85 people attended worship.[9] Later in the century there was a stark contrast between the morning and evening services. A former Minister

---

[7] Hallam, David J. A., *Eliza Asbury, her cottage and her son*, Studley, 2003, Chapters 1-4.

[8] Ibid, p 85.

[9] *Draft history* found in church files 3 November 2017, handwritten note, undated.

recalled 100 to 120 in the evenings, but much smaller services in the mornings led by a Mr Harris for the period 1864 and 1867. There were many "difficulties which prevented attendance". At some point the chapel closed as a Congregationalist cause with the communion service plate and chalice left with Mr and Mrs Wilkins who lived nearby. Mr Wilkins worked as a gardener for a Mr Butler. There was also a Mrs Bunn who was very helpful.[10]

The chapel was taken over by the Methodists, even though it continued to be in the ownership of the trustees of Carrs Lane Congregational Church in Birmingham. There is some evidence it was rebuilt by the Wesleyans but on ordnance survey maps from 1885 onwards it was described as an "Institute".[11] The "Institute" or "Reading Room" was in the management of one "leading spirit", the late Mr Soutter, an old Handsworth Methodist.[12] This Methodist use of the building went into decline and by 1916 had stopped altogether.

---

[10] Letter from Mr C. Hotchkiss to Miss L. Powell, 20 February 1918.

[11] "A History of West Bromwich" by Baugh, C.C., Greenslade, M.W., and Johnson, D.A. Being an extract from the "Victoria History of the County of Staffordshire Volume XVII", London, 1976, reprinted by Staffordshire Libraries, Arts and Archives, 1987, p 69.

[12] "The Chronicle", 20 June 1908, West Bromwich, p 7.

The Congregationalist Revival

By 1916 the Chapel or "Institute" was closed when Miss Tryphena – known as Lillian - Powell, a daughter of a former preacher at the Chapel in its Congregationalist days, came to live at the cottage on Newton Farm. She made enquiries and was advised to contact the Congregational Board.

They suggested she carried out a canvass in the surrounding area to find out what support there was for the chapel to reopen. Sixty-one adults were interested, plus four possible Sunday school teachers and twenty-five scholars. This was reported to the Board who sent a five-man deputation to inspect the premises. They were met by Miss Powell and her nephew. The Board then assumed responsibility for the cost of some repairs and decorations.

The very first meeting of the new congregation took place on Saturday 11 August 1917 when Miss Powell provided a tea party. This was followed by a public meeting chaired by Frank Allen, a councillor, whose grandfather, Mr Thomas Powell of Londonderry, Smethwick, possibly Miss Powell's father, had been involved in the first Congregational Chapel.

The following Sunday, worship recommenced and the Newton Congregational Church was reborn. The service was led by Conrad Hotchkiss who had been pastor fifty years before. There were a hundred people present, and a freewill offering amounted to £2.0s.10d. Miss Powell undertook the jobs of secretary, treasurer, with oversight of the Sunday School which commenced the following week with thirty scholars and eight teachers. A few weeks later oversight was assumed by Mr Frank Allen.[13]

Membership grew rapidly and by 1918 there were ninety-one members with eighty-three attending communion. Pastoral oversight was given by the Rev Martin Roberts MA of Daggers Lane. Miss Powell continued as secretary, assisted by Mrs Frank Allen and Mrs Arthur James (junior) with Thomas Powell acting as Treasurer. [14]

The new congregation threw their energies into building up the church. There were sales of work, a scout group, a choir, a Monday afternoon women's social hour, harvest festivals, and an adult school. Early on they made the decision that communion would be distributed in small individual glasses rather than a common chalice. By 1920 they were able to appoint their first Minister, the Reverend Whitehouse. They also had to deal with very practical issues: there was a shortage of coal, problems with lighting the building and withdrawal of the use of a well in a nearby cottage.

---

[13] Notes in the Church Meeting Minute Book, *1917-1932*.
[14] Church Roll and Communion Register 1917 – 1929 (records incomplete after 1920).

However, the word "success" appeared in church minutes on several occasions.

The new building and the Allen family

By 1927 members realised that the old Institute building was no longer suitable for the needs of a growing church in a growing community. A church meeting gave the deacons authority to "look round for a site in view of future developments, and when found to bring forward for a final resolution by the church".[15]

Developments continued in the old Institute building. In 1927 electric lights were installed. It was agreed that Miss Powell be invited to switch on the lights on the first occasion they were used.[16]

Since the inception of the revived Congregationalist cause Miss Powell had been supported by her nephews Harry Allen of Beechwood, Great Barr and Frank Allen of Saxondale, Bristol Road, Edgbaston. The Allen brothers were wealthy business people. Harry was connected to Marsh and Baxter, the pork butchers. Frank owned Eagle Transfers, a printing company. The minutes and communion records for the 1920s show that Harry was the more active of the two brothers.

---

[15] Church Minute Book ibid, minutes for meeting 6 February 1927.
[16] Ibid, minutes for meeting 16 October 1927.

The Allen family had long associations with the Congregational denomination. Frank and Harry's parents had been active trades people in West Bromwich and had been connected to the Ebenezer Church which met in Old Meeting Street before the family moved out to Newton. Their mother Elizabeth Mary Allen was a "remarkable woman and a woman of very commanding presence......a perfect lady in every respect, and although she had an aristocratic bearing she was possessed with a heart of gold. In fact....she was known as the 'Lady Bountiful' of Carters Green and always possessed a ready ear for the poor and distressed, and that characteristic of benevolence and generosity she had transmitted to her children...." [17]

The Allen family made several gifts to the revived cause, for example providing a baptismal font and being active contributors to the flower rota. However, it was the provision of the site and new building where they really made their mark.

A church meeting in December 1929 was delighted to be told that Frank and Harry Allen had offered the congregation the opportunity of buying a piece of land on the opposite corner of Hamstead Road and Newton Road for a new church. It was twenty yards by thirty yards, giving a total of six hundred square yards. The

---

[17] "New Church for Great Barr. The Allen Memorial" *The Free Press*, West Bromwich, 11 December 1931. Her full name was Mary Ann Elizabeth Allen (email G.Hartley 27 November 2017).

cost would be £100 which the church had to raise themselves within two years. Once that amount had been reached the Allens would hand over the deeds to the plot and return the £100 as a nucleus for a building fund. The meeting accepted with "heartfelt thanks" this "magnificent offer".[18]

The members of the church started a vigorous fundraising campaign. The Ladies' Social Hour and the Sunday School both played their part.[19] There was a bazaar which raised £259, other sources were approached including the Scott Trust. The fund eventually reached £563 but was a long way from the target figure for building the new church.[20]

Plans were drawn up by Albert Bye LRIBA, an architect in West Bromwich. He proposed a two-floor building with the chapel area on the upper floor being accessible from Hamstead Road with a guildhall underneath, accessible from Newton Road.[21]

Then a special meeting of the church was called. The Allen brothers offered to pay for the new building in Newton provided that in memory of their mother and father, it was called "The Allen Memorial Congregational Church, Newton Road". The Church

---

[18] Ibid, minutes for meeting, 15 December 1929.
[19] Ibid, 17 March 1930.
[20] Ibid, *The Free Press.*
[21] Bye, Albert, *Proposed Newton Road Congregational Chapel, Great Barr, West Bromwich*, architectural drawing, 20 June 1929.

placed on record "our grateful thanks to the "Allen Family" for their many generous gifts and constructive service and devotion to the cause of Christ in Newton."[22]

The pledge by the Allen brothers was worth £4000. That would have been the equivalent of more than £250,000 in 2017.[23]

Work quickly began on the new building. Foundation stones were laid by Elizabeth Allen's grand-children on 7 December 1931.[24]

A meeting of members was held in the new guild room on Monday 19 September 1932 when several gifts were formally handed over. These included the building itself but also stained glass windows, a communion table, a pulpit, Bibles, hymn books, flower vases, pews, crockery, lych gate, and much more. Most of these gifts were given in memory of a loved one and duly acknowledged with various plaques.[25] The church was therefore more than a memorial to Elizabeth Allen, but for a whole community.

---

[22] Ibid, minutes for meeting, undated, but signed as correct 22 June 1931.
[23] Bank of England, *Inflation Calculator*, http://www.bankofengland.co.uk/education/Pages/resources/inflationtools/calculator/default.aspx, downloaded 30 September 2017.
[24] Ibid, minutes for meeting, Monday 7 December 1931; Ibid, *The Free Press*.
[25] Ibid, minutes for meeting, 19 September 1932.

The opening ceremony took place the following day, and normal worship began the following Sunday and finally ended on Christmas Day 2017.

The Allen family continued to take an active interest in the church and the accounts show that they provided a substantial income to the church over many years. Both Harry and Frank were made Deacons for Life. After they died their cremated remains, together with other members of their families, were interred in a memorial garden at the front of the church. These were removed shortly before the church closed in 2017 and reburied in Shropshire.

A flourishing new church

The church continued to flourish in the new building. By 1933 they appointed their first full time Minister on an annual stipend of £180.[26]

The church's status as a centre of community activity was recognised in October 1933 when it was formally registered for the solemnization of marriages.[27] The deacons agreed that the first couple to be married at the church would be presented with a Bible.[28]

---

[26] Ibid, minutes for meeting, 26 February 1933
[27] *Superintendent Registrars certificate for the registry of a building for the solemnization of marriages therein*, No 25983, 24 October 1933.
[28] `ibid, minutes for meeting, Sunday 12 November 1933.

By the end of 1933 the church created a Junior Fellowship to attract young people to the morning service.[29] However, this was not particularly well attended. [30]

In 1936 the church had its first change of full time Minister. The church did not have a "manse", the name given by non-conformist churches for the home of ministers and their families. Once again the Allen family came to the rescue: Frank Allen offered to buy a house in Pages Lane with a plan for the church to repay the cost over the following eight years, with the Minister living rent free.[31]

The church at war

Sunday 3 September 1939 saw the outbreak of war between Britain and Germany. This had a great impact on the life of the church, though thankfully it appears that the congregation suffered only one casualty.

In March 1940, a meeting was held to see what could be done to provide comforts for men on active service. This was in response to an appeal from the Mayor of West Bromwich for churches to form working parties for this purpose. There were twelve women prepared to

---

[29] Ibid, 3 September 1933.
[30] Ibid, 26 April 1935.
[31] Ibid, 29 June 1936.

14

form a "Ladies' Working Party for the Provision of Comforts for Members of H.M. Forces".

A handwritten notebook survives showing activity until November 1941. Sometime after the war a pencilled note was added saying that the working party met each fortnight on a Monday until 1945 when hostilities ceased. They made 1260 garments, "adopted" a prisoner of war and made contributions to the Red Cross.[32]

Members were called away on various forms of national service which resulted in much smaller attendance at church meetings.[33] The guildhall was used by the Air Raid Precautions Wardens and a request made for use of the church as a feeding centre in case of emergency to which the church agreed.[34] There were clearly some problems with the ARP occupation of the guildhall and by August 1941 agreement had been reached for the church to be compensated for their use.[35]

The shortage of people at the church was leading to some difficulty in it's administration, so much so that it in 1942 it was decided to suspend deacons' meetings and replace them with a smaller "executive".[36] Scouts and cubs continued to meet with membership at twelve

[32] Westwood, Knitting Class, notebook 1940 – 1945.
[33] Minutes of Deacons Meetings 1929-1945, minutes for meeting 4 July 1940.
[34] Ibid, 22 March 1941.
[35] Ibid, 1 August 1941.
[36] Ibid, 14 March 1942.

and fifteen respectively. Conscription had taken a toll on the Youth Fellowship with just six left. The Junior Fellowship of seventeen continued.[37]

There was only one casualty commemorated in the church, that is for Lt. Peter M. London MBE of the North Staffordshire Regiment. He died on the 19 September 1944 and is buried at Leopoldsburg War Cemetery.[38]

After the war – a golden age

Long-time member Doreen Ward told an oral history project in 2012 what life was like at the Church in the immediate post war period:

"In the 1940s and 50s there were lots of things going on in the church, like youth clubs. All sorts of things. It would be used continually. My friend was in a dramatic society and she said, 'Come and see me'. And told me where the church was. So, I came here. I came here and watched the stage and I said I wanted to join that, so I came and joined."[39]

---

[37] Ibid, 6 April 1944.

[38] *Commonwealth War Graves* website search facility https://www.cwgc.org/find-war-dead/casualty/2109803/london,-peter-morris/, downloaded 1 November 2017. A memorial plaque at the church wrongly described Lt London as a holder of the OBE rather than the MBE. His appointment was listed in the *London Gazette* on 12 September 1944 (email G.Hartley 25 November 2017)

[39] *Voices of Great Barr* – part of the Birmingham oral history project https://greatbarr.wordpress.com/amenities/churches/newton-united-reform-church/ downloaded 1 November 2017.

In the 1930s and the war years formal adult membership hovered around 40 – 50,[40] by 1953, that had risen to 85.[41] Each Deacons' meeting or Members' meeting would report some deaths or transfers to other churches but nearly always these losses were made up by the introduction of new members. Church business meetings would attract up to thirty members.

The Annual General Meeting in 1955 paints a vivid picture of church life. The treasurer reported that there was a bank balance of £296 and that a new envelope giving system would help increase income. The Secretary outlined the main events of the year which included a financially successful garden party. A gift day for the organ fund had been "an outstanding success". There were some problems with the monthly whist drives but these could be remedied by forming a special committee. The sheer size of the church and the various activities led him to warn that "if we want a strong church and congregation, a wider and more concentrated effort must be made to bring everyone into contact with one another and so foster a full fellowship within the church".

The Ladies' Class reported that they met each fortnight on a Monday afternoon. Attendance was good and a visiting speaker gave a short address. There was a

---

[40] Membership book, 1928-1946
[41] Church Membership Roll, 1953. Among those listed were Mr. and Mrs. Searle of Asbury's Cottage, a link with the first home of non-conformity in Great Barr.

Christmas party and a Ladies' Day when services would be conducted by a visiting woman minister. Between thirteen and twenty joined a monthly Ladies' Sewing Class which produced goods to be sold at the Christmas Fayre. The Ladies' Guild reported that they met regularly, numbers were small, but increasing. The Men's Guild reported that they were not strong, and not increasing "very much" but they enjoyed helping to organize the whist drives. The Choir was always in need of new members, but the hope was expressed that they would be good singers.

The Sunday School had gone from strength to strength with 250 children on the roll and increasing. There was an urgent need for more teachers and they were hoping to use the scout hut for seniors to relieve the overcrowding. A Young Newtonians group had been formed with a programme of handwork, beetle drives, square dancing and games. There was no one present from the scouts or guides at this particular meeting, but we know from other reports during the 1950s, that these too were thriving with brownie and cub packs for the younger children, and guide and scout companies for the older children. The Youth Fellowship reported that "their numbers had increased considerably and that they were enjoying a very good period. They had helped out at the garden party, had an outing and held several dances. The meetings included indoor games, panel games, and competitions".[42]

---

[42] *Minutes of Meetings* 1945-1964, AGM, 15 March 1955.

After the Allens

The Allen brothers had endowed the Church and were a major influence from the inception of the church. Frank Allen had died in 1949, Harry Allen, after a long period of ill health, died in 1968. Members of the family continued to play a part in church life but gradually leadership fell to others.

By the mid-sixties problems with the building began to emerge just as the church embarked on the building of an extension to the guild hall. Woodworm was found in the supporting beams to the roof.[43] A restoration fund was set up and loans obtained from the Staffordshire Congregational Union to undertake "essential work".[44]

Despite these setbacks, the church members were enthusiastic for the new extension. This would be on the ground level, and provide a new entry porch, a twenty foot by thirty foot room with partitions to divide it into three, a serving hatch into the main hall, and new changing rooms. The new building would have a flat roof.[45] To facilitate access a two yard strip had to be purchased to the west of the building. There was considerable optimism that funds would be realized

---

[43] Deacons' Meeting, 10 January 1966.
[44] Church Members' Meeting, 5 September 1966.
[45] *Proposed Extension to Guild Room, Allen Memorial, Newton Road*, Simms and Gifford LFRIBA, architects. Architectural drawing, undated.

from increased lettings. More loans would be required and suggestions were made for fundraising.[46]

The work was completed by July 1969. The Treasurer reported that the financial situation "looked bleak" but that it was better than the previous year. The total cost was £7200, leaving the church with a debt of £2500.[47]

During the 1960s and early 70s the church was changing. Full adult membership stood at 69, but there was considerably less recruitment. Income from offerings were static, attendance at the Ladies' Class was "fluctuating", a small number of men met each Thursday and combined their meeting with odd jobs around the church. The Junior Youth Club had been suspended, the Senior Youth Club met each Monday with 24 boys and girls, there were 40 "regulars" at an old-time dancing club, the Sunday School had 104 children with 13 teachers. Both the brownies and the guides were full with waiting lists.[48]

Worries about money led to increased fund-raising activity with some innovative ideas such as a mock wedding, a Dutch auction, and a bazaar which included a fortune teller and a fancy-dress witch.[49]

---

[46] Minutes 1968-1977, Church Meeting, 26 September 1968.
[47] Ibid, Church Meeting, 29 July 1969.
[48] Ibid, Annual General Meeting, 30 April 1971.
[49] Ibid, Bazaar Meetings, 23 June 1971 and 6 September 1971.

The departure of the Allen family in day to day activity inevitably had an impact on the church but it continued to serve the Newton community, especially the young people who attended the Sunday School and uniformed organisations. During the 1970s there was to be the welcome addition of a play group, part of the growing movement for pre-school education.[50]

A change of name and organisation

The 1970s were a time of tremendous change for the Congregationalists. They were under heavy pressure as falling church attendance, migration and demographic movements impacted on their work. In the 1960s it was suggested that the Allen Memorial Church should be amalgamated into just one church with seven other nearby Congregational churches. When the idea was first discussed the grouping would have included four churches which had closed by 1970, leaving just Salem, the West Bromwich Congregational Church and the Allen Memorial, which voted overwhelmingly for the plan.[51]

At the same time active discussions were taking place with a view to the Congregationalists and Presbyterians in England and Wales joining together to form one united church.[52]

---

[50] Ibid, Deacons' Meeting, 28 February 1972.
[51] Ibid, Special Church Meeting, 16 May 1971.
[52] Ibid.

For the third time, the church had to change its name. The Deacons put forward two suggestions: "Great Barr United Reformed Church (Allen Memorial)" and "Newton Road United Reformed Church (Allen Memorial)". A church meeting decided on the latter. One other innovation by the new denomination was that the name of the church leadership was to be changed from "Deacons" to "Elders".[53]

"Holding our own"

The first Annual General Meeting in 1974 of the renamed church was told by the Minister that they were "holding our own" compared with other churches. Reports submitted to the meeting reflected the Minister's cautious optimism, with just one or two exceptions. The flower rota "was going steadily along", the Ladies' Monthly Class had "some good meetings", but the Men's Fellowship were not meeting. The Junior Church (a new name for the Sunday School) was "going along nicely", the Old Time Dance group were "doing well" and "holding their own", the choir were practicing for various events but would like the men to join them for Whit Sunday. One very encouraging development was that the new playgroup was full with a waiting list.
[54]

---

[53] Ibid, Church Members Meeting, 24 April 1972.
[54] Minutes 1968-1977, Annual General Meeting, 4 March 1974.

Problems with the building continued to emerge with another outbreak of dry-rot. Additional loans and gifts had to be sought to repair windows. [55]

A reminder of the Church's links with the community came in 1988 when a commemorative plaque was unveiled to remember the miners who lost their lives in the 1908 Hamstead Colliery pit disaster.[56]

By the mid 1980s many activities continued but there was growing concern about the future of the church. The Church Secretary reported his concerns about weekly giving and the Sunday School to the 1989 Church Annual General Meeting. The Sunday School report to the same meeting underlined these concerns as they had done for several previous years. They reported "another happy year, but numbers do fluctuate between about 18 one week and to 5 or 6 the next. The older girls have calls on their Sundays by schools lately". A "girls' club" had been formed a few years before but numbers had dropped. The luncheon club was still going as were the various ladies' meetings and the playgroup.[57]

A table of membership had been kept in the minute book. Remarkably it showed an increase in membership between 1979 and 1989 when it rose from 78 to 89.

---

[55] Ibid, Church Meeting, 26 June 1986.
[56] Ibid, press cutting from an unidentified newspaper, hand dated, "May 88" inserted on page 156.
[57] Ibid, Annual General Meeting, 14 March 1989.

This was in sharp contradiction to what was happening elsewhere in the country where church attendance and membership was in long term decline. On paper, this was confirmation that the church could continue to say that they were "holding our own"[58]

"Just slowly fade away?"

Early in 1990 the Church members were shocked to find that the Ladies' Monday Class was to stop meeting for the first time since 1918. This led to considerable discussion about the future of the Church.

The Church Secretary repeated some of his warnings to the previous year's AGM but more starkly. He noted that the Church was struggling to connect with young people "of whom we are desperately in need" to introduce them to "Christian faith and worship....The only source of young people were the uniformed organisations, which, although they are attached to the church, are not part of it...[because] they choose to hold separate services". It was "very noticeable during the last 12 months that a 'generation gap' made itself felt". He identified the difficulty of finding younger volunteers to support the luncheon club as an example of this gap.

He continued. "Our membership is declining, the bulk of them are aging, our regular number of worshippers bear no relation to the official membership figures. We

---

[58] Ibid, immediately after the A-Z pages, unnumbered.

have no young people to speak of and few children in our Sunday School. What does the situation auger for the church? Well, we as a church will not close down – suddenly – but if our membership figures dip too low we will not be in a position to sustain a Minister......therefore we will just slowly fade away."[59]

The following year the Elders undertook a review of the Church membership roll and removed 25 names. The uniformed organisations, the scouts and guides, decided that they would prefer to continue to hold their church parades separately. A Ladies' Fellowship was reintroduced and met monthly. Sunday School attendance remained static as did a monthly Girls' Club. Tellingly these three reports were written by the same person. A considerable amount of effort, time and money had been required to make the building secure.[60]

Later accounts show income streams from a lunch club, a dance club, a flower club, a karate class, a 'latchkey' project, a mothers and toddlers group, an over 60s club, and a slimming club. There was no report about these activities to the relevant church meeting: the building had become a venue for other people's activities and the relationship had become commercial, with rent

---

[59] Ibid, Annual General Meeting, 5 March 1990.
[60] Ibid, Annual General Meeting, 6 March 1991.

providing about a third of church income, rather than as part of a wider fellowship.[61]

Sunday Schools are always a good indicator of a church's future. Having pre-adolescent children in the church community inevitably means there are parents in their late twenties and thirties, who would be the elders and office holders in the future. During the 1990s the annual report from the Sunday School demonstrated the difficulties they were facing.

Each year the Sunday School superintendent would report that they were happy, but expressed concerns that the number of children attending was static.[62] When figures appear in the minutes they show just how precarious the future of the Sunday School really was: by 1997 attendance averaged about seven children.[63]

The following year the superintendent submitted a hand-written report which simply stated:

"The numbers are most disappointing and I am at a loss to know what to do to contact more children to come along. The few children we do have seem to enjoy our meetings together but I would welcome any suggestions."[64]

---

[61] Ibid, Accounts to Annual General Meeting, 5 April 1997.
[62] Ibid, Annual General Meeting, 7 March 1992.
[63] Ibid, Annual General Meeting, 5 April 1997.
[64] Ibid, Annual General Meeting, 28 March 1998.

A few years later, the Sunday School at Newton Road, in common with those of many other local churches in the region, had faded away altogether.[65]

By 2017 the congregation was less than a dozen people, all of whom were over 60, many much older. When confronted with the prospect of fundraising to make the building safe, they had no alternative but to close altogether, with the last service scheduled for Christmas morning.

Newton Road URC in Context

The story of the Newton Road United Reform Church, especially its closure, needs to be seen in a wider context. There is no doubt that those who offered to finance the new building in 1929 thought it would be there for many years, hence their decision to have their cremated remains and that of their families interred in the garden. This was shared by other members of the Church who commemorated their loved ones with memorial plaques.

There was every reason to be optimistic about the prospects for the Church. In the 1920s and 1930s the population in the civil parish of Great Barr was growing rapidly. Although it was still largely rural, between 1920

---

[65] The author is a Methodist Local Preacher in a nearby circuit and a similar pattern has been observed there: most Sunday Schools were down to a handful of children in the 1990s and then stopped meeting altogether in the 2000s.

and 1930 the population had increased from 2,232 to 3,294. Despite the war, over the next 20 years it quadrupled to 12,648 by 1951 and that growth continued into the 1950s and 1960s.[66] By 2015 there were 18,840 adults registered to vote in the two local government wards which covered Great Barr.[67]

There were issues with the building. It was on a very constricted site on two levels and against a bank at the bottom of which water collected. Problems with damp, woodworm, dry rot and the brickwork quickly emerged. The entrance from Newton Road was very isolated and enabled vandals and burglars free access to do their damage. That would have been a huge drain on resources, even for a well-endowed church.

However, the major factor in the decline and eventual closure of the Church was the changing spiritual and social landscape: Britain became a more secular society and there was a dramatic drop in church attendance everywhere. This process was well underway very early in the twentieth century, but accelerated towards the end.

---

[66] *A vision of Britain through Time Website,* Administrative Unit Great Barr Ch/Tn/CP http://www.visionofbritain.org.uk/unit/10272865/cube/TOT_POP downloaded 13 November 2017.
[67] Elector_Analysis_by_Electoral_Area_2015.pdf, Sandwell MBC downloaded 26 November 2017. Totals were 8,965 for Newton Ward and 9,875 for Great Barr and Yew Tree, over 18 year olds registered to vote.

The decline was especially felt in the free churches, including the United Reformed denomination. When the Allen Memorial Church was opened in 1932 the umbrella Congregation Union claimed 483,599 members across Great Britain. By 1950 that had fallen to 388,696. On the eve of the creation of the United Reformed Church, 1970, membership was 262,018.[68]

In 1980 Sunday church attendance was about 11.1% of the population of England, by 2015, it was down to 4.7%. The URC mainly operated in England. Total attendance across all URCs in England was believed to be 188,300, by 2000 it fell to 112,000, by 2015 down to 33,100.[69] If anything, the Newton Road Church fared slightly better than its wider denomination.

Church histories often celebrate the buildings or the pioneers. Those who built the church deserve lavish praise and we should thank God for their vision.

The congregation of Newton Road in later years offer a different perspective: for more than 40 years they battled against overwhelming odds to keep their Church open to serve their community and their God. Many of

[68] *British Religion in Numbers* website, Table: Comparison of selected churches 1767-1970 http://www.brin.ac.uk/figures/churches-and-churchgoers/other-churches/ downloaded 13 November 2017.
[69] Ibid, Table: Total Church Attendance in England 1980-2015 http://www.brin.ac.uk/figures/church-attendance-in-britain-1980-2015/ downloaded 13 November 2017.

them remained committed well into the closing years of their lives.

They provided an important community space for young people, especially the uniformed organisations.

They opened their hearts and building to their neighbours offering food, fellowship and company to many elderly people.

They provided a safe space for play groups and mothers and toddlers.

They were heroes who battled to live out their faith against overwhelming odds.

May the community of Newton be thankful for their commitment.

And may God bless them.

Their mission is now complete.